# D'Nealian

# Writing

# Practice

# For Kids

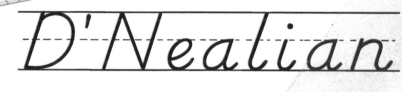

# Teaching guide for
# D'Nealian Writing Practice for Kids

- This writing practice is appropriate for grades kindergarten through second.

- A variety of D'Nealian font styles are used to give your student multiple ways to learn, trace, and then practice writing D'Nealian style.

Teaching style for guidance

Tracing style for practice

Practice style, with larger dot to remind student where to begin each letter

Practice style with no guidance

- Basic uppercase and lowercase letters are the basis for this teaching material, however higher level words are provided if your child shows interest in tracing and writing those words as they learn.

- If your student resists writing the higher level words allow them to focus only on the basic alphabet first.

- Space is provided for students to practice writing about themselves.

- When the student has reached a comfortable level of accomplishment in their D'Nealian writing practice they can advance to tracing and writing the silly sentences provided as the second portion of this practice book.

- Schedule learning and practice time when your student is engaged and interested.

- Make learning time fun and rewarding for your student. The silly sentences are intended to bring humor into learning, and also aid in teaching your student about alliteration.

Happy writing!

airplane

ant

alligator

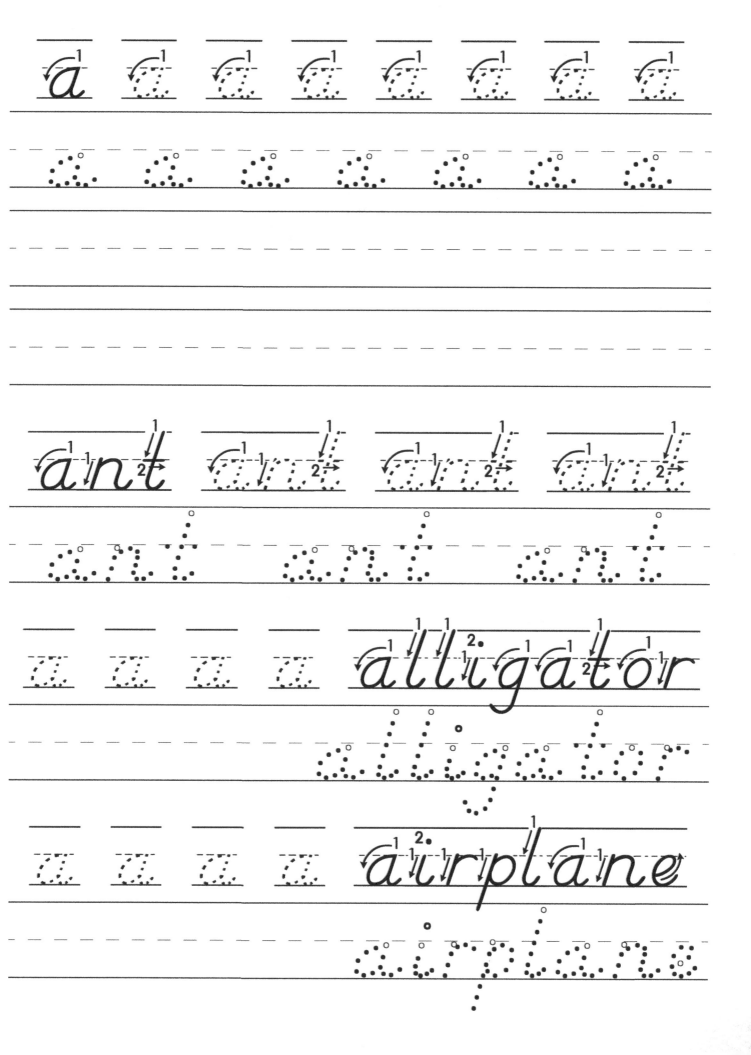

butterfly

banana

bird

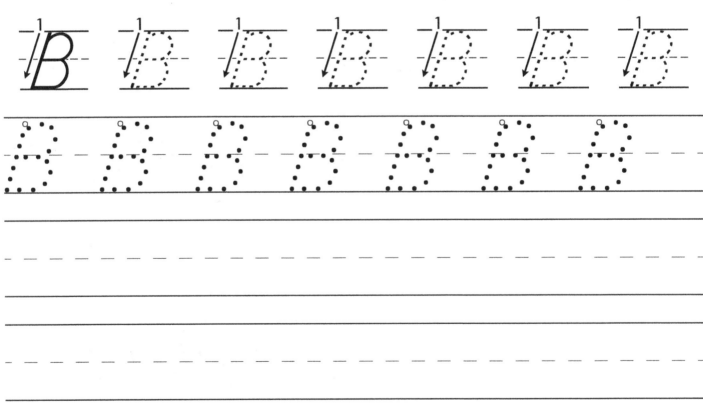

b b b b b b b b

b b b b b b b b

bird bird bird

bird bird bird

b b b b banana

banana

b b b b butterfly

butterfly

Cc

cat

cake

caterpillar

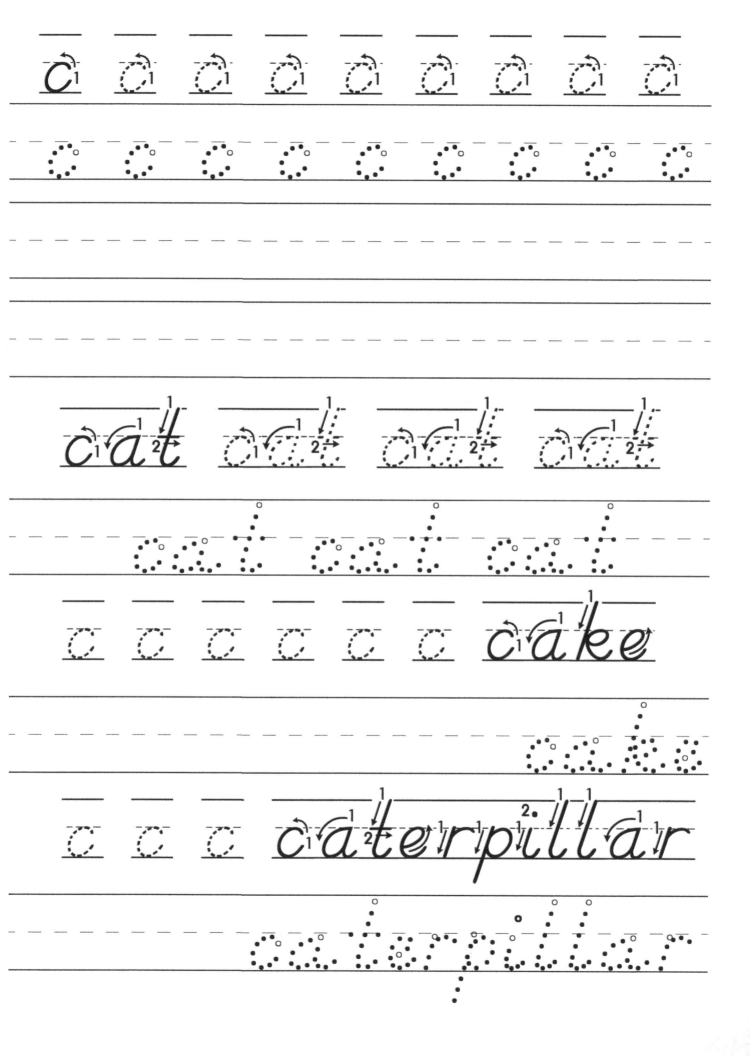

# D d

dog

doughnuts

dinosaur

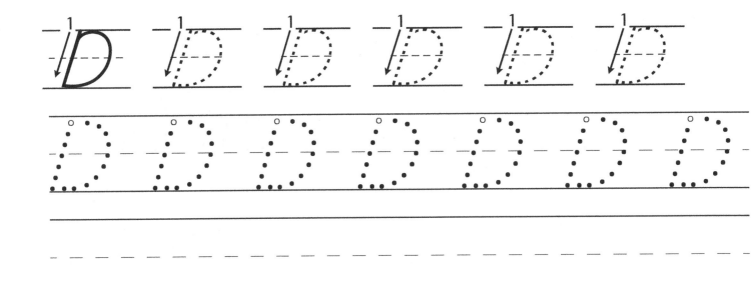

d d d d d d d d

d d d d d d d

dog dog dog dog

dog dog dog

d d d doughnuts

doughnuts

d d d d dinosaur

dinosaur

elephant

egg

eggplant

e

egg

eggplant

elephant

fish

frog

fork

*Gg*

*grapes*

*giraffe*

*guitar*

# H h

house

helicopter

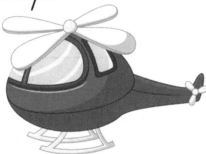

hippo

h h h h h h h h

hippo hippo hippo

house

helicopter

# I i

igloo

ice cream

iguana

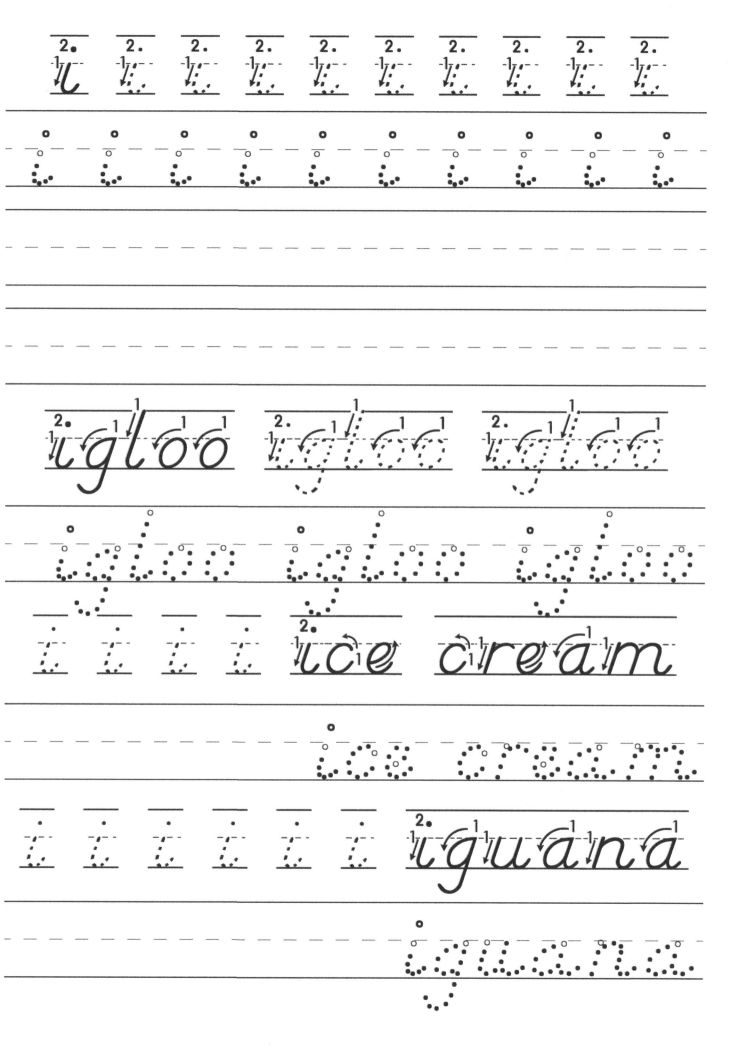

Jj

jellyfish

joker

jaguar

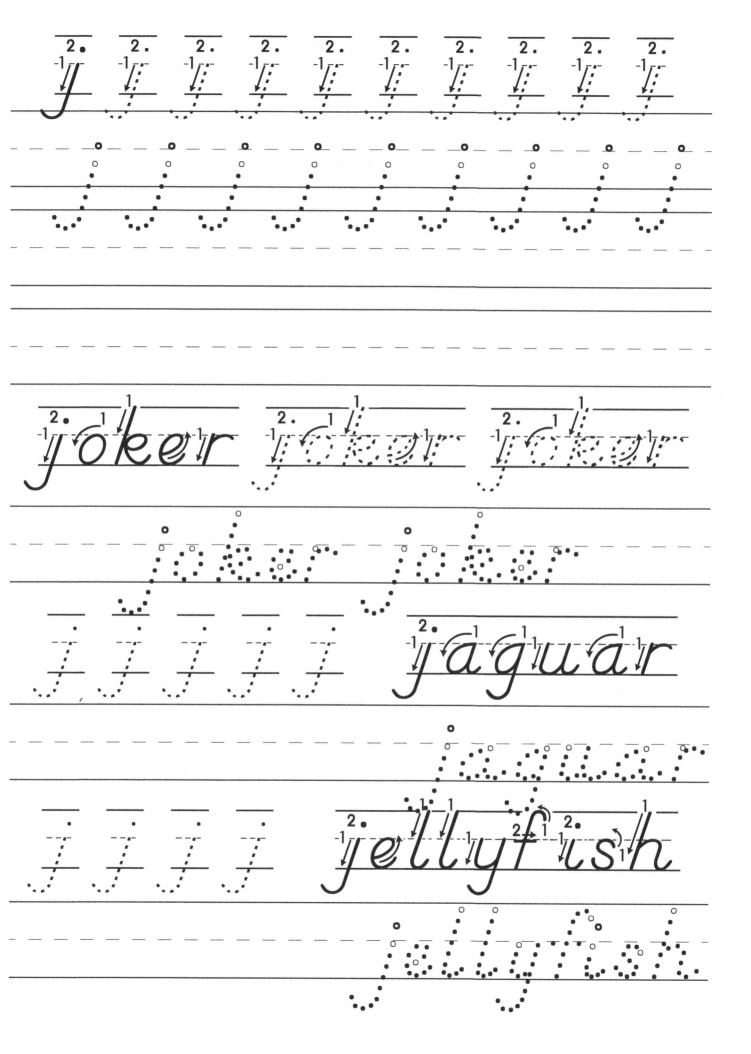

kite

kangaroo

koala

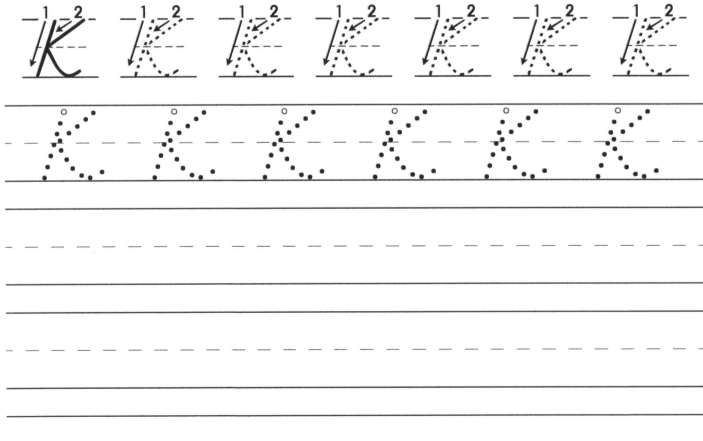

k   k   k   k   k   k   k   k

kite   kite   kite   kite

k   k   k   k   k   k   koala

k   k   k   k   kangaroo

lion

lollipop

lemon

*l l l l l l l l l l l*

*l l l l l l l l l l*

*lion lion lion*

*lion lion lion*

*l l l l l l* *lemon*

*lemon*

*l l l l l l* *lollipop*

*lollipop*

mushroom

mouse

monkey

m m m m m m

m m m m m

mouse mouse

mouse mouse

m m m monkey

monkey

m m mushroom

mushroom

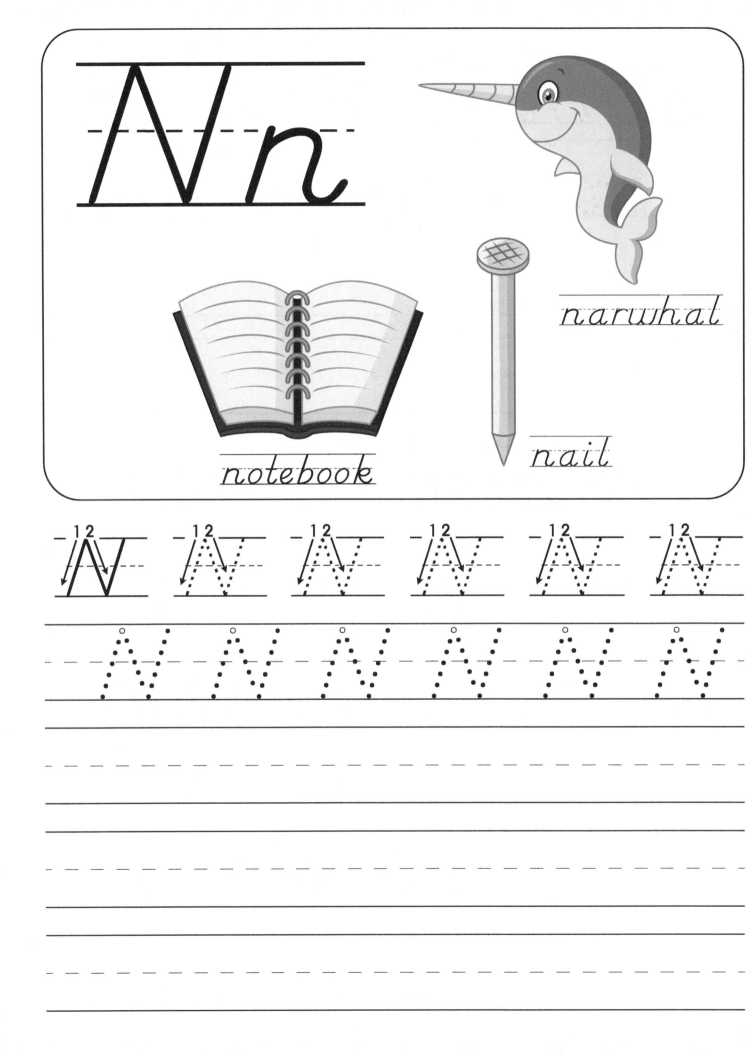

notebook

narwhal

nail

# n

n n n n n n n

n n n n n n n

nail nail nail

nail nail nail

n n n n notebook

notebook

n n n n narwhal

narwhal

octopus

owl

orange

pig

pear

pizza

p p p p p p p p p p

P P P P P P P

p p p p p p p **pig**

p p p p p p **pizza**

p p p p p p **pear**

quail

queen

quill

raccoon

rabbit

rocket

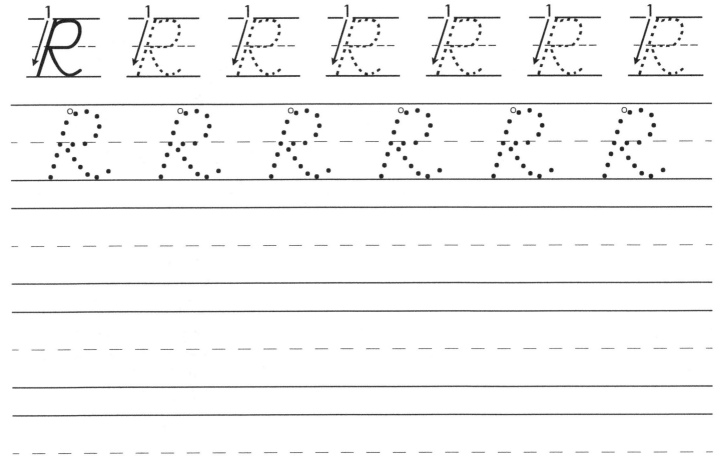

r r r r r r r r r r r

r r r r r r r r r r

r r r r r r rabbit

rabbit

r r r r r r rocket

rocket

r r r r r raccoon

raccoon

sponge

snake

sun

tire

toothbrush

tiger

*umbrella*

*ukulele*

*unicorn*

vulture

vase

violin

windmill

walrus

whale

# Xx

xylophone

x-ray fish

x-ray

X x x x x x x x x

x x x x x x x x

x-ray x-ray

x-ray x-ray

x x x x-ray fish

x-ray fish

x x x x xylophone

xylophone

yak

yo-yo

yam

y y y y y y y y

y y y y y y y

yo–yo yo–yo yo–yo

yo yo yo yo

y y y y y y y yak

y y y y y y yam

yam

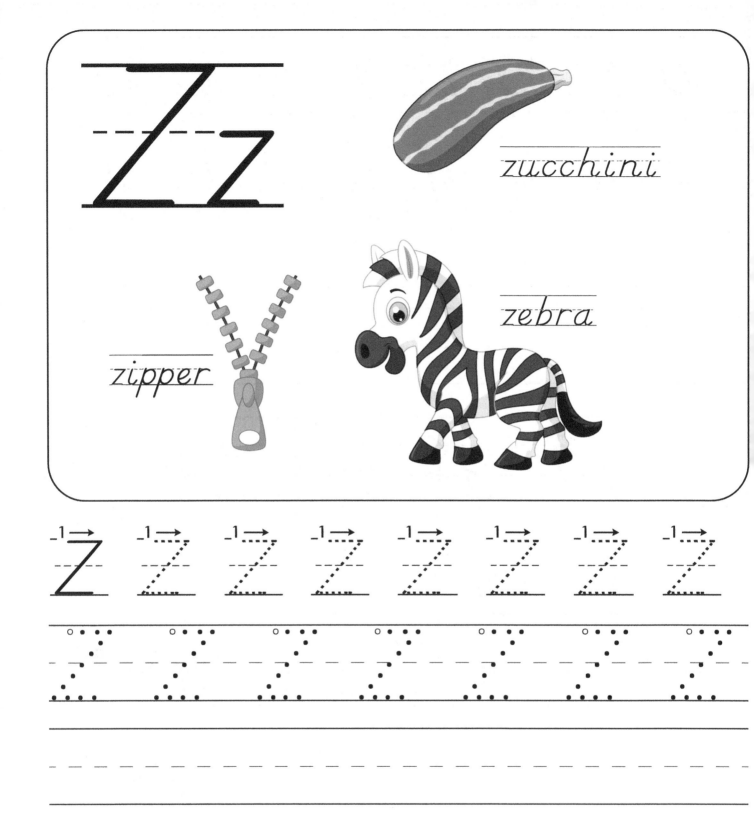

zucchini

zipper

zebra

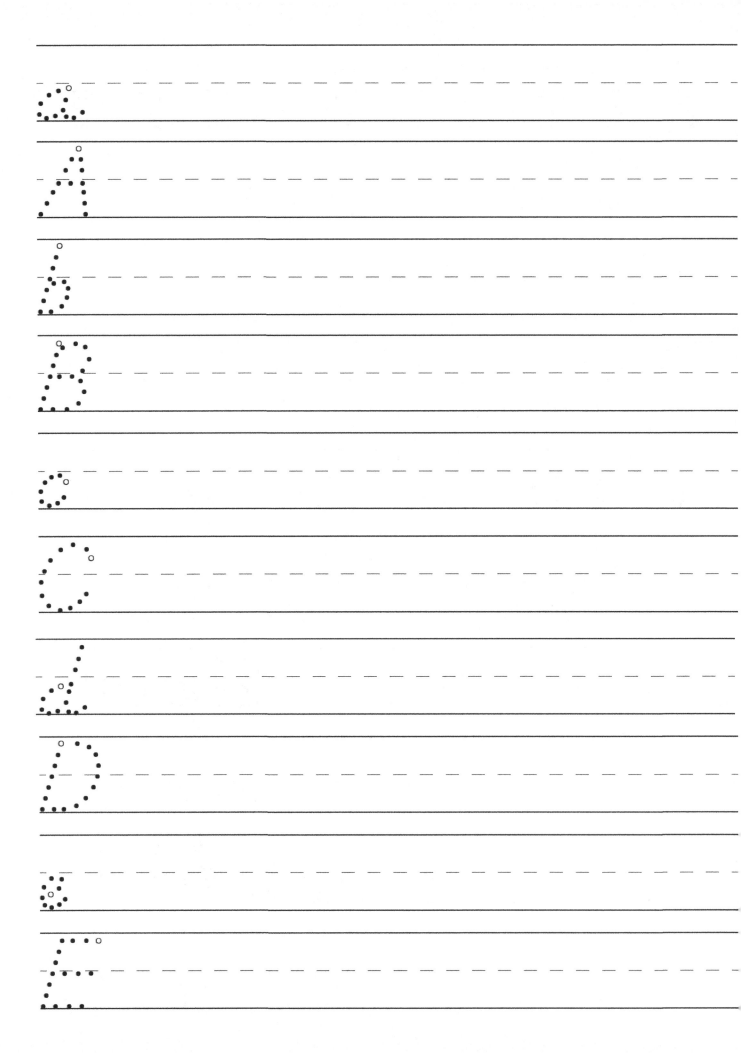

My name is:

I am _____ years old.

My eyes are:

My hair is:

I have a pet.

My pet's name is:

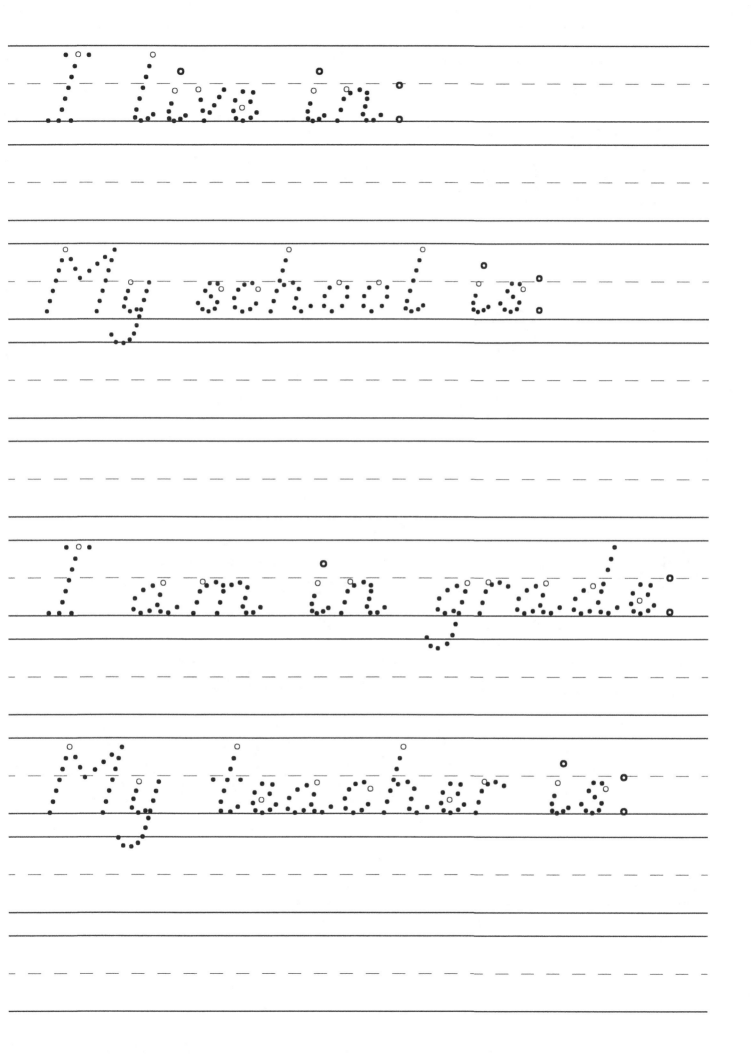

I live in:

My school is:

I am in grade

My teacher is

Aa

airplane

ant

alligator

Andy alligator and Alice ant arrived to Alaska by airplane.

Andy alligator and Alice ant arrived to Alaska by airplane.

butterfly

banana

bird

Bobby bird and
Bella butterfly
baked banana
bread for
breakfast.

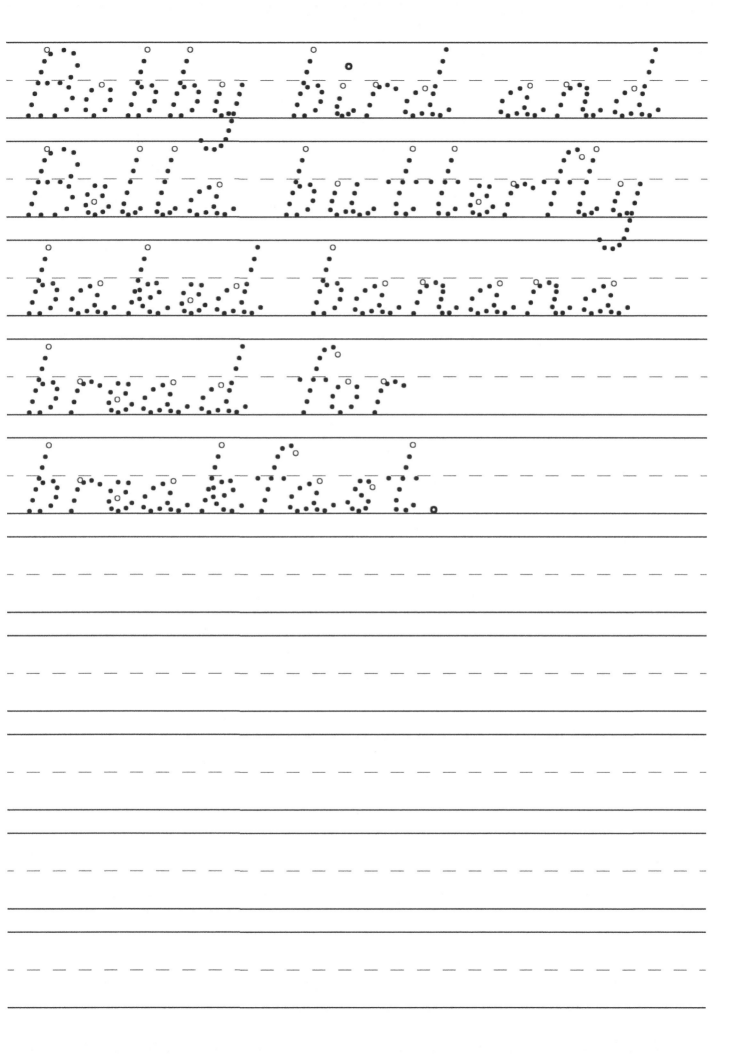

Bobby bird and
Bella butterfly
baked banana
bread for
breakfast.

# Cc

cat

cake

caterpillar

Cal caterpillar carried a cake to Caitlyn cat's cozy cabin.

Cat caterpillar

carried a cake

to Caitlyn

cats cozy

cabin.

D d

dog

doughnuts

dinosaur

Dory dog does not like doughnuts but Delores dinosaur does.

Dory dog does
not like
doughnuts but
Delores
dinosaur does.

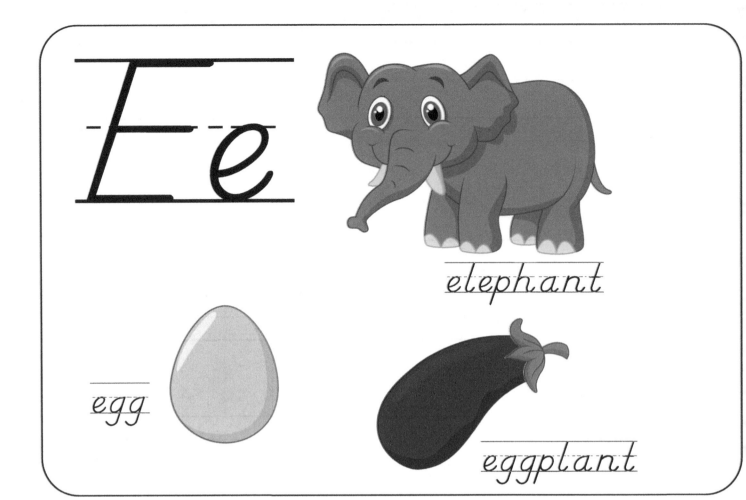

E e

elephant

egg

eggplant

Eddie elephant expected to find an egg in his eggplant.

Eddie elephant elephant
expected to find
an egg in his
eggplant.

Ff

fish

frog

fork

Freda frog's fork
fell off the table
and landed on
Frank fish's
forehead.

Freda frog's
fork fell off the
table and
landed on
Frank fish's
forehead.

# Gg

*grapes*

*giraffe*

*guitar*

Greta giraffe
ate grapes
while playing
the guitar.

Greta giraffe ate grapes while playing the guitar.

house

helicopter

hippo

Hannah hippo
flew her
helicopter high
above her house.

Hannah hippo

flew her

helicopter high

above her house.

*I i*

igloo

ice cream

iguana

Isaac iguana insisted on eating ice cream inside an igloo.

Isaac Galang

insisted on

eating ice

cream inside

an igloo.

J j

jellyfish

joker

jaguar

Jojo joker invited
a jellyfish and a
jaguar to do
jumping jacks.

Jo Jo Joker
inverted a
jellyfish and
jaguar to do
jumping jacks

Kk

kite

kangaroo

koala

Kevin kangaroo
and Kate koala
flew their kite
in Killarney.

Kevin kangaroo
and Kate
koala flew
their kite in
Killarney

Ll

lion

lollipop

lemon

Lucas lion licked
his lemon
flavored lollipop
and laughed
out loud.

Lucas Leon
licked his
Lemon flavored
lollipop and
laughed out
loud.

M m

mushroom

mouse

monkey

Mabel monkey
made mushroom
pie for Marley
, mouse's mom.

Mabel monkey

made

mushroom pie

for Marley,

mules & men.

narwhal

notebook

nail

Nancy narwhal
used her nail
nose to write in
her notebook.

Nancy marshal
used her nail
file to write in
her notebook.

# Oo

octopus

owl

orange

Octavia octopus
offered Odelia
owl an orange.

Octavia octopus offered Odalia owl an orange.

pig

pear

pizza

Pippa pig
preferred pears
over pizza.

Please put

preferred pairs

over plain.

quail

queen

quill

Queen Qiana
quickly made a
quill from a
quail feather.

Queen Qiana

quickly made a

quilt from a

quail feather.

raccoon

rabbit

rocket

Ricky rabbit rode
in his rocket to
rescue Rhonda
raccoon.

Ricky rabbit

rode in his

rocket to rescue

Rhonda

raccoon.

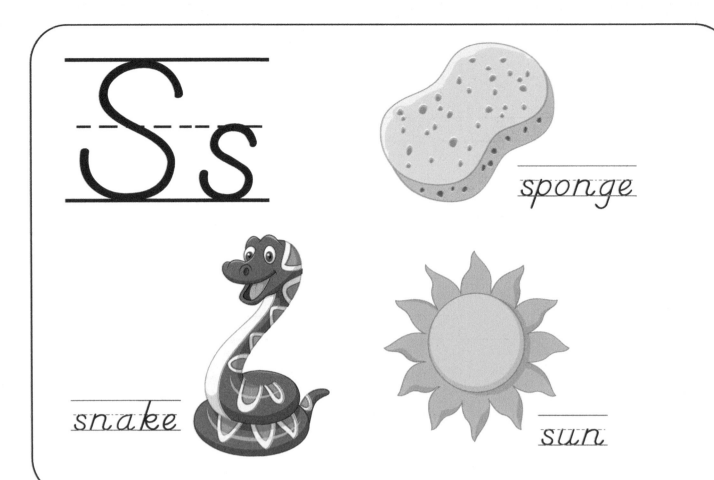

sponge

snake

sun

Selina snake soaked up the sunshine like a soggy sponge.

Salina snuck snacks soaked up the sunshine like a soggy sponge.

# Tt

tire

toothbrush

tiger

Tina tiger tried
to polish her tire
with a tiny
toothbrush.

Tina tiger tried
to polish her
tras with a tiny
toothbrush.

*U u*

*umbrella*

*ukulele*

*unicorn*

Ula unicorn sat under an umbrella to play her ukulele.

the unicorn

sat under an

umbrella to

play her

whistle.

vulture

vase

violin

Vincent vulture
stored his violin
in a voluminous
vase.

Vincent vulture

stored his

violin in a

voluminous

vase.

windmill

walrus

whale

Willy walrus and Wanda whale lived under a whirling windmill.

Welly walrus
and Wanda
whale lived
under a
whirling
windmill

xylophone

x-ray fish

x-ray

Can an x-ray
fish play the
xylophone while
getting an x-ray?

Can an x-ray

fish play the

xylophone while

sitting an

x-ray

Yy

yak

yo-yo

yam

Yegor yak thinks
yams are yummy
and yellow yo-yos
are fun!

Your web

things yarns

are yummy

and yellow

yo-yos are fun!

zucchini

zipper

zebra

Does Zane zebra's stripes come from zippers or zucchini?

Does Zorle

zebra's stripes

come from

flippers or

flooding?

# Congratulations!

_____

You have learned to write D'Nealian letters.

Thank you for working so hard. Give yourself a high five!

Made in United States
Orlando, FL
18 October 2024

52825022R00096